ZACHRONYMS™

DAVID ZACH | funny words for funny times

cover illustration by matt zumbo
cartoons by jim rowden

For information, please contact:

Innovative Futures Press
225 E. St. Paul Avenue, Suite 303
Milwaukee, WI 53202
414-278-0461

ISBN # 1-891630-00-8   LCCN # 97-77834

Although the author and publisher have made every effort to ensure the accuracy
and completeness of information contained in this book, we assume no responsibility
for errors, inaccuracy, omissions, or any inconsistency herein.

This book is a parody, and any slights of people, places, products, or organizations are
unintentional. As a matter of fact, glowing endorsements from the author of said people,
places, products, and organizations are available for cash or trade.

First printing May 1998

Attention corporations, educational groups, and professional organizations:
Quantity discounts are available on bulk purchases of this book for educational or
fund-raising purposes. Special books or book excerpts can also be created
to fit specific needs. For information, please contact Innovative Futures Press.

dedication

WILLIAM JOSEPH SANDERS

"*pop*"

1898-1989

humor is hereditary

contents

Zachronyms are acronyms – made-up words using the first letters in a phrase to make a new word, like saying POSSLQ instead of Persons of the Opposite Sex Sharing Living Quarters or BYOB for Bring Your Own Beer. Most acronyms are invented by people in big organizations who are trying to save time, but who end up sounding like they're speaking Martian. Maybe they are–it would explain a lot about these modern times.

Zachronyms are not from Mars–they're from right here on planet Earth. Some Zachronyms tell you about your fellow earthlings and what they're thinking and doing. Other Zachronyms are just for laughs. All together, Zachronyms will give you a new set of words that better explain money, work, love, and life at the millennium.

Enjoy this book with friends and strangers alike. You'll share some good laughs, learn some great new words, and be amazed that so many of the people you find out there are in here too. And be sure to look in the back of the book to find out how to send in your own Zachronym!

FAMILIES

...using the liberal definition

dinks | double income, no kids

dinkys | double income, no kids yet

ditkas | double income,
two kids around someplace

dinkwads

double income, no kids,
with a dog

nikes

no income, kids everywhere

double income, college kids	**dickies**
one income, no kids	**oinks**
single income, no kids	**sinkers**

sitcoms	single income, two children, outrageous mortgage
sickos	single income, couple of kids
silkies	single income, lots of kids

yummies

young, upwardly mobile mommies

taffies

technologically advanced families
fully interested in electronic stuff

single income, one or two ex-spouses	**sintex**
double unemployed, numerous kids	**dunkies**
parents in nursing home, kids in school	**pinkies**

fobys | fathers older, babies younger

podwags | parents of dinks
without any grandkids

nebnos | new baby, no sleep

rombies

really old mothers with babies

fiestas | families intent on establishing shared time and stability

muddies | middle-aged, unhappy divorced dads

poops

pet owners outnumbered by pets

YOUTH

slackers	students lacking all common knowledge
slopies	students living off parents' income
swampies	students wasting mom & pop's income

skippies

school kids with income and purchasing power

naughties	needing an understanding grown-up to help tame immature sensibilities
smackers	societal morons allowing children to keep evading responsible standards
swoggies	students waiting on graduation gifts
flyers	fun-loving youth en route to success

ckones

rynical kids of the ninaties

jerks	job-evading, reckless kids
farts	fathers against rowdy teenagers
swine	students wildly indignant about nearly everything

cabies

caffeine-addicted busy students

ELDERS

oggies

on-the-go grandparents

disgruntled old people | **dopies**

expecting lots despite
evading responsibility | **elders**

barely able to see | **bats**

peepers	poor elders expecting prosperity and early retirement
premies	premature retirees expecting more income
zippers	zero-income post-professionals enduring remaining savings

fossils

faithful old secretaries still intensely laboring

toppies
treacherous old people perpetrating
ill will, evil, and sarcasm

frugal, responsible,
unpretentious mature persons | **frumpies**

confident, old, financially fit
elders reveling in savings | **coffers**

woofies | well-off, over fifty

warts | wealthy and retired
by their sixties

whordes

wealthy husbands who are
old and run down

LIFESTYLES

...and other attitudes

faldos

fast-lane dropouts

young urban failures	**yuffies**
middle-aged student radicals	**masries**
home-oriented moderates with ethically renewed standards	**homers**

scumies	socially conscious, unless money's involved
shirleys	stars have interesting reincarnated lives, escaping your situation
oompies	opting out of the melting pot

cooties
children out of
the early sixties

dwamies

dead white american males

colors

conflict only lengthens our resolve to separate

waffles	wholly addicted to fast food, likely to eat seconds
low cals	losers of weight craving another loaded serving
hearts	healthy exercisers against the right to smoke

huffies

heavy users of fast food

readers	*respecting education is a detail of employment and real success*
tikes	*thought i knew everything*
lifers	*losing intelligence fast, embracing the remote*
spams	*stupid people avoiding mental stimulation*

spores

stupid people on rented equipment

uppies

unbelievably peppy people
inevitably expressing stupidity

stupid people in need of
an education at reform school | **s p i n e r s**

doing only obligatory functions
and using up space | **d o o f u s**

barely using mental skills | **b u m s**

twits

those who insist they're special

least-appealing way you employ revenge	**lawyers**
pain in the ass	**pita**
vengeful, over-taxed electorate rejecting spenders	**voters**

WORK

...is overrated

prumpies	previously radical upwardly mobile professionals
wumpies	worthless upwardly mobile professionals
vuppies	vulgar urban professionals

grumpies
grim, ruthless, upwardly mobile professionals

lumpies

losing upward mobility professionals

pregnant urban professionals	**puppies**
rural upwardly mobile professionals	**rumpies**
cunning upwardly mobile professionals	**cumpies**

slumpies	slowly losing upward mobility professionals
duppies	deceived about upward mobility professionals
dumpies	downwardly mobile professionals

yippies
young, indicted professionals

yupsids	young urban professionals, seriously in debt
marpies	middle-aged rural professionals
gin rummies	government income, resisting upward mobility
dopes	dual occupations, perpetually evading success

disillusioned, relatively ordinary
professionals preferring independence | **droppies**

newly inspired baby boomers leaving
employers to rely on selves | **nibblers**

without having an income that
exceeds the cost of living,
lots are really scared | **white collars**

callers

cellular abusers loudly letting everyone
realize their status

doing their required occupation, | **d r o n e s**
neglecting everyone

retired on active duty | **r o a d i e s**

losers at managing everything | **l a m e s**

beepers	busy executives engaged in pretending electronics reveal superiority
bowties	big, overweight, totally ineffective executives
peppies	perfect examples of the peter principle

bitch

boys, i'm taking charge here

MONEY

...and the lack of it

maffies	middle-aged affluent folks
maddies	middle-aged debtors
fibbers	financially incompetent baby boomers evading realistic savings

buddies

baby boomers under deep debt

ouchies

on unemployment, couch habitant

lombards

lots of money, but a real dirtball

dumbies | dual mortgages and broke

spellers | stupid people expecting luxurious
lifestyles, except reality sucks

nitwits | new income that would have
increased total savings

greepies

greedy rich executives with excess perks

LOVE

...and its alternatives

dins

double income, no sex

digs

double income, great sex

sins	single income, no sex
ninies	no income, no sex
sissies	singles into safe sex
shut ins	stay-at-home, unadventurous traditionalists immobilized by non-safe sex

people opposed to people enjoying sex	**popes**
naive encounters with those outside of normal sexuality	**newtons**
lousy at managing the opposite sex	**lamos**
nearly everyone's recently divorced	**nerds**

feelers | fully expecting every love to evolve into a relationship

laborers | lonely, aging boomers oblivious to reality, expecting relationship success

internets | intense nerds thinking emotions refer to nonessential things

dosidoes

dating outside the species inspires
drop on evolutionary scale

bagels	barely getting enough love to survive
gals	getting a lot less support
gents	genuinely elegant, nice, talented, and successful

new age gals	**nags**
sensitive new age guys	**snags**
men attempting to really try to increase emotional sensitivity	**marties**

remotes

relying on electronics more than emotions

feminists loving insecure men	**flimies**
women encouraged by any vague example regarding sensitivity	**weavers**
women insisting that no guys are needed under their skirts	**wingnuts**

babes | beautiful attributes bring on endless staring

wealthers | women engaged again to losers that have economic resources

girls | giving in results in lower status

wammies

women on a mission
to marry income

bummers

beautiful, upwardly mobile, but married

women having intense negative expectations regarding sex	**whiners**
women in need of sex	**winos**
women in need of great sex	**wings**

may days

man of your dreams? are you sure?

switchies

stupid women intending to change him

doggies

determined, outgoing guys intent on eventual success

average nice guys, experiencing love before sex	**angels**
husbands unusually nice, kind, and sexy	**hunks**
grown-up men behaving immaturely, especially about sex	**gumbies**

carbons	commitment avoiders really believing they only need sex
worms	womanizing, obnoxious, repulsive men
scum	socially confused, useless men
boys	boring, obnoxious young studs

studs

so talk to us, dorks

slugs | social losers using guilt to score

snots | single, nasty, and out for themselves

yobbies | young, obnoxious bores

fully unaware nobody notices
inept efforts to seduce | **funnies**

boys assuming racy females like
inept efforts to seduce | **barflies**

bastards | boys artful at seductive tricks,
are really deceitful scum

savants | single adventurers with vasectomies
anticipating nooooo troubles

grabbers | guys really annoying babes
by expecting recreational sex

testies

teans expressing sexual tension in every situation

NAMING NAMES

...would a rose by any other name...

cpa | certified pain in the ass

golf | gentlemen only, ladies forbidden
legend says this is the original definition. i doubt it.

pms | pardon me, sybil

ems | earns money sleeping

peta

people for eating tasty animals

iowa | idiot out wandering around

i owe the world an apology

i know there's one for illinois, but it's not going in this book!

alitalia | always late in takeoffs,
always late in arrivals

doesn't ever leave the airport | **delta**

i am chairman of chrysler | **iacocca**
corporation of america!

at chrysler, it was known as:
i am chairman of chrysler
corporation. amen!

bmw | break my windows

cadillac | can't always drive in lanes
like another car

dodge | drips oil and drops grease everywhere

fix it again, tony | **fiat**

fix or repair daily | **ford**

found on road dead

for old, retired drivers

generally mediocre cars | **gmc**

mercedes

most every red cent eventually
disappears, extinguishing savings

men express really cocky egos
driving expensive sedans

old ladies driving slowly, making others
behind infuriatingly late every day | **oldsmobile**

pretentious, obnoxious, rich slobs
can have everything | **porsche**

such an arrogant bastard | **saab**

hey, wait a minute, that's what i drive!

bill

bubba is living large

see page 105 if you need a hint for this cartoon

highly inexperienced,
left-leaning,
academically righteous
yuppie

highly intelligent
lawyer
leading a revolution
for you

hillary

newts	newly emerging wealthy traditionalists
democrats	deceptively eloquent, most oppose capitalism, reality, and taxpayers
gop	greedy old people
	going over the people

when i need data output
without speed   **w i n d o w s**

satan posing as meat   **s p a m**

futurists | foolishly unaware that ultimately reality isn't so trustworthy

about the zach in zachronyms

David Zach is one of the few professionally trained futurists in the United States, with a master's degree in Future Studies from the University of Houston-Clear Lake. Dave makes his living by speaking before business and education audiences who want to hear someone talk intelligently about the future in a down-to-earth, entertaining manner. Zachronyms began appearing in his presentations over 10 years ago and took on a life of their own.

In case you're wondering, Dave does not use tea leaves, astrology, or any of the psychic hotlines. He's never met Shirley MacLaine. He's never even been Shirley MacLaine. Dave's just an ordinary guy having a lot of fun asking the age-old question:

Where do we go from here?

Dave's four brothers, Jim, Rick, John, and Mike, insist that he make it clear that Zach rhymes with Bach. After years of struggling to get people to pronounce it correctly, they are not about to let Dave ruin all of that. You can pronounce Zachronyms any way you like.

If you liked the book, you just might love the talk

To paraphrase Mark Twain, everybody talks about the future, but no one does anything about it.

Dave Zach's a guy who *is* doing something about the future— he's helping people to understand trends, and how to balance change with tradition—all with a touch of humor and thoughtfulness. And audiences love it. Here is just a sample of what they're saying:

"...clearly the hit of the week with our customers!"
— Lorin M. Stearns, Program Manager, IBM

"...superb!...witty, funny and insightful!"
— Allie Chamberlain, Conference Manager, American Petroleum Institute

"I got many thanks for putting you on our program.... Thanks for making me look good!"
— James H. Camp, Ed.D., North Carolina Community College System

**For information about having David Zach
speak to your group please contact:
John Reede
Nationwide Speakers Bureau
310-273-8807
www.nationwidespeakers.com**

Qualified meeting planners are invited to contact

their favorite speakers bureau or call 414-278-0414 to learn how

to have Dave speak to their groups.

Who knows, maybe we'll be quoting you next time.

Visit our website at www.innovativefutures.com

contributors

Bill & Debra Bryant, Rick & Marcia Janezic, Timothy Leary, Ronald F. Malan, Lyle & Julie Maryniak, Bill McGinnis, David B. Phillips, Traci Phillips, Patty Pritchard, Rich Wright, Stacy Van Alstyne, Peter H. van Dorsten, Jeane Wegner, and Barbara Wurtz.

Special thanks to the team who helped put this book together: Susan Heymann (public relations), Jean Kaiser (marketing), Terri Lonier (advice and inspiration), Janet Menz (office management), Barb Paulini Nelson (graphic design), Chris Roerden (publishing consultant), Marilyn & Tom Ross (printing consultants), Jim Rowden (cartoons), Kim Wilson (editing), Marissa Zumbo (cute little baby on cover), and Matt Zumbo (cover illustration and uncle of cute little baby on cover). Building a book is an amazing amount of work, and these people made it all worthwhile. The journey is part of the reward.

Finally, a great big thank-you to Don Dooley of the Metropolitan Milwaukee Association of Commerce. Don writes the MMAC Hotline newsletter and through the years has published some of the acronyms. One day, without warning, he called them Zachronyms. And the rest, as they say, is the future.

Hi Dave! Here's my suggestion for a new Zachronym.
Please use it in your next book, Bride of Zachronyms.

_____

_____

_____
please print your name clearly here.

_____
address or e-mail

[] Yes, I crave publicity and would love for you to credit my name in your book.

[] No, I'm an intensely private kind of person, and would shrivel up in shame if
you used my name, but feel free to use the acronym.

[] Sorry, but as I am in the witness protection program, I cannot give you my real name.
But of course you are free to use the acronym.

signature: _____

please read both sides of this page before signing.

Now the legal stuff from my gifted and expensive attorneys: By sending your contribution to me, you agree that you are sending it by your own free will, you are over 18 or have your parents' permission, you are releasing and assigning all rights to it (including any copyright or trademark rights), you're letting me use it for whatever purpose I want, and, if you like, I can credit you as having submitted an acronym to join this collection.

That being said, the next book, *Bride of Zachronyms*, is waiting patiently for your acronyms—and you don't want to keep her waiting, now do you?

Snailmail: Bride of Zachronyms,

Innovative Futures Press,

225 E. St. Paul Avenue, Suite 303

Milwaukee, WI 53202

Faxmail: 414-223-4757

Email: acronyms@zachronyms.com

Visit the Zachronyms website: www.zachronyms.com

gifts

get it from the source

Looking for that perfect gift? Can't find this book at your local bookstore? Did the dog chew up your last copy? Have you "borrowed" this book from someone else and are feeling slightly guilty?

Then just order copies of Zachronyms, fresh from the source.

Yes, please send me ____ copies of

ZACHRONYMS
funny words for funny times

at $8.95 each plus $2 shipping and handling per book. (Wisconsin residents add 5% to total order.) I will patiently wait up to four weeks for delivery.

Name _____ **mail to:**

Organization _____

Address _____

City State Zip _____

Phone ( ) _____

My check or money order for $ ____ is enclosed

Charge my [] VISA [] MasterCard   Card Number _____

Exp.____ Signature _____

Innovative Futures Press,
225 E. St. Paul Ave, Suite 303
Milwaukee, WI 53202 or
call (888) 243-1887 or
fax to (414) 223-4757